Removal Acts

Removal Acts

Poems

ERIN MARIE LYNCH

Graywolf Press

This publication is made possible, in part, by the voters of Minnesota through a Minnesota State Arts Board Operating Support grant, thanks to a legislative appropriation from the arts and cultural heritage fund. Significant support has also been provided by the McKnight Foundation, the Amazon Literary Partnership, and other generous contributions from foundations, corporations, and individuals. To these organizations and individuals we offer our heartfelt thanks.

Published by Graywolf Press
212 Third Avenue North, Suite 485
Minneapolis, Minnesota 55401

www.graywolfpress.org

Published in the United States of America

ISBN 978-1-64445-253-0 (paperback)
ISBN 978-1-64445-254-7 (ebook)

2 4 6 8 9 7 5 3 1
First Graywolf Printing, 2023

Library of Congress Control Number: 2022952331

Cover design: Adam B. Bohannon

I turn your head
stone flat
to eat off it

you ate then
turned to dirt
I flatly eat

my head turns
off filled with
flat stones

I turn
into you fully
headfirst

CONTENTS

Removal Acts

FOREWORD

TO THIS I COME

From the claim I lay to those no longer with me—

From the desktop folder to which I drag
        another .jpg, another .mov—

From syllables kept beneath the tongue—

From boiled eggs, dry chicken, unsalted greens—

From the day I learn an uncle had spoken Dakota—

From telling my mother, who replied *I never knew*—

From waking into sudden ringing silence
        on my thirtieth birthday, in another new home,
        in another new state—

From punctuation to punctuation—

From the taste that lingers when the meal is gone—

From dandelions I joined into a circle when I was younger—

From this uncle, who died with no one to speak to—

From his grandmother, buried in Standing Rock—

From the .jpg of her headstone, carved with her
        name, *Elisabeth*, and the years of her life—

From my stomach walls collapsing, night after night—

From the hunger inside me, surging toward
        a love over whom I no longer held claim—

From stamen to root—

From the prairies of the Dakota homelands,
        where Elisabeth lived when she was younger—

From settlers who claimed that land for statehood—

From the eaves of my new home, where a pair
        of pigeons perched, encroaching—

From the .mov of the two of us I couldn't bring
        myself to delete, in which I saw myself
        smiling—

From lo even the briefest joining of earthly things—

From dandelion seeds settlers scattered
        across the continent to recreate home—

From the English language and its shifting
        definitions, its rule of law—

From 1862—

From *Hungry men will help themselves*, said a chief,
        declaring war—

From that war, from the exiled survivors—

From the smell of an uprooted dandelion,
        and the stains—

From all my mother never knew—

From how could she have known, when no-
        longer-knowing is the State's project—

From a baby, according to a tribal telling,
        snatched from her mother and dashed
      to the ground—

From official records of *few deaths* along the march—

From these *few*, each a name their family knew—

From the dash, which elides—

From the prairies where Elisabeth died, in another
        new home, in another new state—

From the long unknown years of her life—

From the dandelion, a slightly bitter green,
        with waxy milk running through—

From stems uprising between us—

From the long no longer—

AFTERWORD

ST. HELENS

I came when called; polished silverware

with blue paste; saw myself in the mirror

then turned away, thinking, *seeing herself*

naked, she turned away; soaked my blood-

stained underwear in the sink; sat silent

at church like moss on a car hood; shut

the shoebox that held a long, dark braid,

severed a century ago by a butcher knife;

waded the culvert down to where it fled;

read about the Vanishing Hitchhiker,

who appears in the back seat, whispers,

St. Helens will erupt in May; let shadows

in my closet press closely, hissing, *show us*

your ugly heart, lift up your shirt; wondered

if ghosts chose to be; lay on my back under

the apple tree; felt the neighbor's shape fall

across me as he said, *nothing like a pretty*

girl reading; was allowed by distance to hide

the volcano, small and cold, with my hand.

REMOVAL ACT

Many of the households in my family keep a portrait of Mato Sabi Ceya, my grandfather's grandfather (great great great). We find this portrait on the website of the museum that has acquired the original. *Acquisition notes: Photographs of North American Indians and miscellanea given to the Department of Ceramics and Ethnography.* We screenshot the image, print it with shitty inkjets, then cut the paper into smaller rectangles measured to fit dollar store

The original in Washington, tol of the A m e r i c a n grandfather's Sabi Ceya had to discuss *D e p a r t m e n t : and the Americas.* of the Oyate, longest. They in my grand- ing) rowed Mato the Atlantic, his ing that ocean. *on display.* Oars waves, they gave sign the treaty He signed, fin- ing, ink mixed streaking down *R e g i s t r a t i o n A m , A 3 9 . 2 3 .* res black-and- his pipe, blan- gaze fixed to his

picture frames. photo was taken DC, capi- ever-expanding Empire. In my telling, Mato traveled there treaty terms. *Africa, Oceania* Of all the chiefs he'd held out (always "they" father's tell- Sabi Ceya into first time see- *Location: Not* pushing back him a choice: or go overboard. gers shak- with salt spray, p a r c h m e n t . *n u m b e r :* Here, in low- white, he holds ket over knees, right (my left).

© *THE TRUSTEES OF THE BRITISH MUSEUM*

USING THIS IMAGE:
SORRY, THIS IMAGE IS NOT AVAILABLE FOR DOWNLOAD

Technique: albumen printing. Up close, I feel the living distance between my forehead and his forehead. Up close, creases under his eyes, hooked arc of his nose, his broad upper lip all dissolve into ink dots. *Asset number 645095001.* Each dot a droplet. Each dot void. Each dot sovereign. The opposite of diminishment: countless dots make up the face of the grandfather we place in every home.

8.5 X 11

Interesting story . . .

       written in red ink
       at the top of my
       mother's paper

           . . . Is this even true?

                 1972—Eighth Grade American Indian Unit

                 even then, her faultless cursive
                 recounting her father's recounting
                 of Sitting Bull's murder

today we learn
to say who we are
in Zoom Dakota class

tiles enclose faces

       COMMAND + SHIFT + A
       unmute

   shapes move through mouths

     Damákhota
     Oregon hemátaŋhaŋ ye
     Tuktédaŋ omáwapi šni ye

           afterward I forget everything

           walking the dog past beautiful
           people lifting weights, stretching
           by the bronze bust of Leif Erikson

glistening populace of the open field
shadows keep casual intimacy
deepen in overlaps

*Homework: What is all the information you can give someone about yourself
and what would your introduction sound like?*

half-second misaligned
perfecting an echo's echo

but my legs are   in running shorts and my face is   on dating apps and I check the
box for   on government forms ergo I am   in any residual sense   phenotypically
slash culturally   slash   in terms of my rearing as well as   in case of receipt of
cultural or academic capital from the largely   establishment that is to say I am   to
any glance   passing or otherwise

        in the documentary
        a fisherman's voice-over

        we are living out long-term genocide

        he slits a salmon
        points to good flesh

the terms of   ness are long-term and to be   is endpoint of every room that has in-
cluded me for being meekly   and legibly

        "finally, there was the groundless shame of the
        inadvertent impostor" wrote Adrian Piper

        (she looked   to the   gaze but wasn't   )

if I wrote in   on   paper
it would look like

FIGURE [?]

Dear unmet. Dear unmeetable. Speaking of mothers. Elisabeth. *Not only that woman whose womb formed and released you.* Sometimes her name is spelled Elizabeth.

It's about placement of the subject in relation to other objects in the arrangement. *Who is responsible for the suffering of your mother.* She traveled at least 492 miles from her birthplace. As I track on Google Maps. And lived through that. Or that. Or that.

Enactment of preordained arguments. Suspicious sheen of a finished poem. *Never believe that a smooth space will suffice to save us.*

Proximity has little to do with love. Kenel, location of her grave. Site of Sacagawea's death, allegedly. Grandpa leaning out the RV in a NAVY VETERANS trucker hat.

Too much blood pooling in my fingertips. *We were beginning a process of reclamation.* For a long time I worried all this was none of my business.

BLOODLINES

assembled above
the shoe rack, past
relations papering
the wall, sutured
with staples. My
eyes scanned up
our tiny photos,
[?] standing
for the missing,
born and dead

formation

[?] – [?]   [?] – [?]

[you] – [you]   [you] – [you]

[?] – [you]   [you] – [you]

[you] – [you]

[me]

suited for flight

FROM THE ARCHIVE OF AMERICAN OBJECT LESSONS

OBJECT NAME:

Self-Portrait of the Speaker in Her Great-Grandmother's Dress

MATERIALS:

Cotton, Cloudy water, Muddy footprints, Large rocks, Barbed wire, White girlhood, Glass beads, Small rocks, Open access, Cattails, Humidity, Search engine, Moth balls

PLACE:

Mni Sota, Fort Yates, Hillsboro, Rex Hill, In the bathroom mirror, Under the hosta's lip, On the highest shelf, Beneath the boxspring, On a USB, East Hollywood, Unknown

DATE CREATED:

March 3, 1863—President Lincoln signs into law "An Act for the Removal of the Sisseton, Wahpaton, Medawakanton and Wahpakoota Bands of Sioux or Dakato Indians, and for the disposition of their Lands in Minnesota and Dakotas."

1910—Camp Fire Girls, an outdoor program for young women, begins in Vermont. The founders model symbols and activities on their idea of Native American culture.

191 [?] —My great-grandmother, Lorena, joins the Camp Fire Girls. She sews a "ceremonial gown," meant to resemble traditional clothing of Plains Indians. Lorena poses for a photo in the dress, paddling a canoe.

1928—My grandfather, Robert, attends St. Bernard Mission School on Standing Rock Indian Reservation. The boys learn to garden, the girls to sew.

1935—Robert's family moves to Oregon. They pawn heirlooms, including regalia, before they go.

1946—Lorena's daughter, Helen, marries Robert. Lorena passes the Camp Fire Girls dress to Helen, who keeps it.

1980—Robert and Helen's daughter, Ann, wears the Camp Fire Girls dress to Cultural Heritage Day at her high school.

20 [?] [?] —The photo of Lorena in her dress is lost, somewhere between houses.

2019—Ann, my mother, finds the dress hanging in a closet. She folds it into a padded envelope and mails it to me.

2020—I set up a tripod and record myself putting on the dress and taking it off, over and over. Watching the footage, I'm startled by how much I look like her.

2023—The Sioux-Dakota Removal Act has not yet been repealed.

the personal   is familial
        is cultural   is
circumspect   is historical
   is direct   is a fradulent
      is antique   is cotton
   is light brown   is
      fringed   is hemmed
   is an embroidered   is
beaded   is folded   is
   treasured   is addressed
      is redressed   is an
         underdressed   is
                  undressing

Addressing now that Cultural Heritage Day. Mom in her room after school. Square room. Hello Kitty poster. She stands by the window. Hair damp at the neck. Is it okay for me to see her. Her as my invention. In her private environment. She's still wearing the dress. Wrinkled at the thighs. Sweat stains. Mustard spot in the shape of a comma. Thick cotton the color of hide peeled from a deer. Old cotton smelling of powder. Hem heavy with beads. From the kitchen the smell of toast burning. Her many brothers laughing in the living room. She can't see all sides of herself at once. Only the tip of her nose with one eye closed. They are laughing too loud. My fear of revealing to herself her own body. Is it okay, Mom. For me to undress you. Only to discard the costume. Outside it is raining. Steady drops rolling from the tips of the ferns. It is a ceremony of a kind. You pull the dress into your fists and over your head. You disappear from me without leaving your room.

FIGURE [?]

Sepia mountain of buffalo skulls. Intonations of a trained narrator. Cross-dissolve. Wipe screen.

I live because you lived through. *How am I to not tell the story has to be told.* As I negotiate, may I address you? I want not to count you as the United States has done.

I lived through. Not what you lived. Nightly crouched by the toilet, two fingers down my throat. I tried and failed to eradicate.

Convulsion, compulsion. *A single specious need to keep what you have never really had:*

Summer air hot like fresh money, sick light on the box hedge leaves, gulls blocking the wind, string of brake lights, playlist titled Unbearable, cloudy water streaming from the faucet, coffee grounds festering in the trash, branches weighed down by wet oranges, a beetle clinging to my headphone cable, its green tectonic back, clouds dividing, replicating, empty street in the dark, a distance of trees and the distance comes closer . . .

Images assumed to be speechless.

KNIFE

Hunger

    [spills]

        from the hole in the maple
          my father fitted
            with a spout

          [fills]

        the kitchen with putrid
      vinegar my mother sprayed
        to kill pantry moths

              [multiplies]

        larvae

      [pushes]

      through her
brown rice

[settles]

in the driveway seams

      concrete cool
      against my cheek

      a landscape
          boundaryless
      unswallowing

petrified set of my lips
belonging to no one

ant
        [crawls]

    in my mouth
    then out again

        [takes]

    sagging fence posts
            leaf blower's roar
    pinecone falling

        [makes]

        my yard
        your yard

    even those words
their checkered texture
    from an airplane

                [empties]

        the allotments
    we left behind

[knows]

who now inhabits that land

    [extends]

an aftermath
of paper plates
at the reunion
in memory

[returns]

ring of cocktail shrimp

white sheet cake
embordered with roses
not a word written on it

they let me hold the knife
I sliced

[divides]

again and again

lengthwise
crosswise

BEFORE RECOVERY

How did I do it? I was a slack
      suit of clothes, a treadmill's
dry tongue lapping itself up.
      More than once, I fed
the dog more than myself. More
      than once, I threw
the kitchen door open to taste
      air: unmowably green,
green of graze, green of let go.
      I counted the caloric content
of air I'd eaten. From hunger
      comes hunger, sharpened.
The butter knife, the bread
      knife. I emptied even
my voice. On my knees
      to pray, I chewed my gums
instead, chewed my mouth
      to shreds. I was the door,
the gash in the screen. I was
      the dog, slipping through.

TO GO THERE

[cool dim of a lecture hall]

                [outside, cherry blooms heavy with bees and their kin]

[someone stepped to the mic, posed a question]

        [the Dakota scholar replied]

        I don't find angst about personal identity interesting or helpful

        [note in my phone: "no point in being fraught"]

You have to go there

        [grandpa said]

        It would be good for you to go there

                        [is all this citation
                        a way to prove
                        my legitimacy]

        Don't forget you come from

        [hand on my shoulder]

        Don't go getting lost

                        [like the CDIB in
                        the file box under
                        my bed, paper, papers
                        sheathed in papers
                        and a flat dead moth
                        pressed open between,
                        no less important]

how connected are you to that side

[a classmate asked]

how much
are you

[?]

[?]

[?]

[legs folded
on its furred
tubular body
in a posture
of patience]

[turns me again to a dog-eared page from *WHEREAS*]:

~~Though I'm told~~ *I come from a small world* [I was afraid of]
[seeming only] *a lifted paragraph from* ~~one or~~ *other book*[s]:

It took many trials before I learned how to knot ~~my sinew thread on the~~ point
~~of~~ my finger~~, as I saw her do. Then the next difficulty was in~~ keeping my ~~thread
stiffly twisted, so that I could easily string my beads upon it.~~ ~~My~~ mother [with]
~~required of~~ me ~~original designs for my lessons in beading. At first I frequently
ensnared many a sunny hour into working a long design. Soon~~ I learned from
self~~-inflicted punishment~~ [not] to refrain ~~from drawing complex patterns,~~ for
I had to ~~finish whatever I~~ began.

I thank [Layli Long Soldier and] *Zitkála-Šá*
as I learn to ~~otherwise~~   [enter the un] *put*:

FIGURE [?]

Stretch of gum revealed when the lips spread. Stale taste after throwing up again. Toothbrush bristles yellowed.

Several repeated actions to reach the point of vomit. How it moves down then up then through. Acid eats and eats. *Satisfied physiological hunger gives way to unsatiable spiritual hunger, a striving for what "it could possibly mean."* Today I decide to die and don't because of the dog's heft at the end of the bed.

I'm searching for a bridge between lineation and lineage, but no bridge is there. We put too much stock in such things, you and I. *And the "we" is always the right mode of address here.* We read, reread the root.

Form, not flesh. Consumed, unconsumed. You know you still retain half the calories. Acid as method. Acid as extract. I know you know.

At a life-drawing class, the model sits naked in a window, artists in the dark outside. I can't write anything where anything but this happens. I envy the dead their past-tense bodies.

SIDE EFFECTS

Fatigue Failure Bloody Libido Acid Mood Diarrhea Irregular Kidney Uneasy Heartbeat Reflux
Decay Ulcers Puffy Pulse Skin Fluctuating Loss Eroded Obsession Tears Facial Constipation

one fixed shot

    Elisabeth walking in a circle

        sky stretched above
           she steadily circles

           where she circled
           now circles

                makes clearer
                nearer

                  and nearer
                  nearer and

                     knowing the way

                          I call out

Cheeks Hands Swollen Anemia Worthlessness Muscle Gum Imbalance Miscarriage Dehydration
Guilt Swings Indigestion Throat Teeth Nails Scarred Sore Dry Brittle Rapid Fluttering Inflamed

IWÓBLU

while water protectors held against rubber bullets, I

glamorized: my illness
romanticized: my ancestors
aestheticized: my politics
idealized: my crush

somebody well-meaning
bet you wish you were there
I nodded but surely felt

too scared of having an
eye shot out of tear gas
of gas masks of snow of
not (shameful) belonging

on a bench on the grounds
of the Seattle Indian Center
looking over the Sound

with white-bright wind
I read how she died in
the *Catholic Sioux Herald*

tawič">u	*wife*
činča	*child*
héna	*there, right there*
čuwita	*to feel cold (used only of animate beings)*
téhaŋ	*for a long time*
iwóblu	*blizzard*
akípapi	*to befall*

I am doing my best
with the online lexicon

feels wrong to even place
the title of this poem

in Dakota, but then
Grandpa you told me

she untied the horses
they survived

frost on nostrils
harnesses quivering

OPENING NIGHT AT THE FLYING HERITAGE & COMBAT ARMOR MUSEUM

Everything is disarmed.
Salvaged fighters hang from tension wire.

Cocktail napkin. Champagne.
Hors d'oeuvres on silver trays.

> Replica bomb roped
>   by red velvet:

> PLEASE DO
> NOT TOUCH

> My right hand used to measure
>   my left wrist daily.

> The goal, a greater
>   dearth of self.

Behind glass, a rat
bulges with batting:

> meant to be filled with TNT
>   and thrown into trenches,
> but never deployed.

> *Dearth.* Almost *death.*

> A flat tone, as if nothing mattered.

The rat emptied of one purpose,
          given another, like a metaphor—

I lick crumbs from my lips.

        A suit of skin
        can be filled, emptied,
        filled again. Ripped,
            split, sewn, thrown.

        Like a metaphor of violence,
        almost violence.

FIGURE [?]

To put on the page things you barely sought to say, even to me. *I can hear you making small holes in the silence.* Barred from material encountering.

But it's my own voice I can't stand. My mother's voice and her hands considered by her to be ugly and the set of her jaw.

How far beyond your mother do you hope to get? And all my love, of hers derivative. Nine bees in a film canister, hard and soft cheeses arranged on a board.

The last poem of mine she read, my mother said, *What an unhappy lady*, and I was flattered she distinguished me from you. *A focus on their suffering, as if to not suffer is to not honor them, to forget them.*

History is narrative. Narrative is a trauma response. Your skin is my coat, made of many thin coats. It took years to make.

EPIGENESIS

The first time the forest burns, I brush ash from the windshield, cover my nose with my sleeve →

My mother stabs herself, sewing a cow print dress with buttons that spell *MOO* →

In a class called Myth & Metaphor, my teacher points to a projection of a brain →

When you see someone in pain, this part lights up →

No way to breathe without breathing it in →

In the beginning we have neither myth nor metaphor, nor the notions of myth and metaphor, nor the brains from which such notions spring →

The shadow of an arm falls across that mottled organ, set alone in space →

MOO → Open lowing, calf calling →

Contented cows stay silent → Dead ones too →

For her I button to my neck, for her I twirl →

Years later, I see new shoots among charred stumps → In the distance a cloud, another fire sweeping → I roll the windows up →

In my brain a word clicks shut → *MOON*, whose gaze pulls every bead of blood closer →

Somehow we survive that too →

my mother ate the worst parts of the meat → her father went to the Mission School → she never heard him say I love you not once → my mother hit me → is that him in the photo with the other children hair cropped close → she never saw him dance → my mother picked at the fatty parts → she hit me again → I heaved into her shirt → her father told me once he had to eat the horses or not at all → she hit me then held my head in her arms → her father wouldn't dance at the powwow → he unhooked his arm from mine and turned away → the drummers kept singing the Victory Song → long slabs of fat left on her plate → she held my head gently →

I do not
believe in
poetry as
solace or
I do not
believe in
my poetry
as solace
for *now*

solace (English)→ "comfort,
consolation" → *solaz* (Old
French) → "pleasure, enjoyment" →
solacium (Latin) → "soothing,
assuaging" → *selh-* (Proto-
Indo-European) → "to reconcile"

cannot be
resolved
with *then*
that seeps
blood down
the creases
of a finger
allowing
the joints
to curl to
pull away

Now I →

open the cedar hope chest
jump at the slam of a door
turn the dog onto his back
miss a planetary conjunction
lift my niece onto my lap

Then I →

let her pull my hair hard
stare into monotone fog
softly scratch his belly
unfold yards of gingham
close my eyes to steady

shhhh, I say, stroking the air around her head → she taught me to scrub cast iron → my

inherited need for it, scalding → nuns taught him to read, taught his brother to fiddle →

her father calls me *Shorty*, calls me *Slim* → it is *a psychic and consequently physical*

truth → my mother raised me with predestination → she liked the water hot, her knuckles

red → her post-post-historical consolation → bits of charred meat rising through gray

suds → particles kept apart, even touching → my niece outgrew the buffalo hide

moccasins → our mothers saved baby hair in envelopes → to remove rust with lemons

and salt → her son had a daughter → her face composed of these events and stories about

→ murky dissolution → emptying the dishwasher, I place a bowl →

within a bowl →

within a bowl →

. . . And so they took him up to Fort Yates and they buried him out there . . . out there close to where Esther lived . . . just . . . the cemetery was there . . . uh . . . [this is Sitting Bull? Sitting Bull died at] *. . . yes . . . Sitting Bull . . .* [Sitting Bull died at Wounded Knee] [but they brought him up to Fort Yates Mom] [oh ok after he died at Wounded Knee] *. . . yeah . . . it was a uh . . . um . . . at any rate . . . so there was . . . the grave was there and it had rocks around the grave . . . huh . . . and it was there and . . . it got so there was a . . . another one beside it that was marked the same way . . . I don't . . . so uh . . . what uh . . . they . . . any rate . . . uh Mobridge is forty miles away but they wanted to use for . . . draw huh. . . .* [they built a monument right] *. . . right built a momument and . . . so . . . they thought . . . so . . . they came in the middle of the night and dug his grave . . . and took him down and buried him outside of . . . outside of Mobridge and . . . but . . . the kids had changed the rocks and I think he's still buried there . . . but any rate . . . they moved the grave of somebody and put him . . . and they celebrate . . . that's part of their celebration each year . . .*

she held my head in her arms →
she held my head against her chest →
she held my head like a ripe melon →
she held my head as joints shook →
she held my head as the jawbone rattled →
she held my head as within sockets eyes rolled →
she held my head → she let me go →

I stoop in the grass, bagging dog shit →

Above my head, a gold medallion tree →

The dog pulls the leash, averts his eyes →

I ask my mother to record her father →

In the video, he breathes in, coughs out →

Memory, like weather, shows up each day →

Seed pods transluce, filled with clusters →

In the video, he gives a new ending →

He's certain the story he told is the way it is →

I have spent too much time quiet →

I have spent too much time talking →

I am learning to save every part of this animal

LIVE STREAM

I'm back looking at the photo of

Her grave while on another screen

Live streaming a rare moonflower

Closed in a Cambridge greenhouse

Single tapering bud about to bloom

At which point Science pollinates

Delicately with a damp paintbrush

Then the scent turns rancid & dies

All this in twelve hours I can watch

From my bedroom where blood has

Dried on my sheets in the mirrored

Shape of a heart I hate that I think

This way searching for beauty in any

Accident the fading stain I have not

Washed out while my smallest screen

Glows with warnings from a watering

App *TAKE ACTION TAKE ACTION*

I try to keep plants alive & succeed

So long as I look at them often with

Steady gaze refocusing on what matters

In the shot for me & 179 other waiting

Viewers the moonflower has not moved

Perceptibly nor have I from this photo

Of her grave timestamped 07/14/04

Below the marble pillar with sunken

Inscription & carved cross there a pink

Blur must be roses I zoom until they fill

The screen head & necks shades of pinks

Secreting their scents amid the long grass

Trampled by whoever in the flesh picked

The roses arranged them left them to be

Preserved by chance at their most open

Rock of Ages

ELISABETH
DIED
FEB.14.1910,
AGED
64 YEARS.

Mother thou art gone to rest
And this shall be our prayer
That when we reach our
journey's end,
Thy glory we may share

❧ ❧ ❧ ❧ ❧ ❧ ❧ ❧ ❧ ❧

MAJHOR

Rock of

_____

_____

our

journey's

share

_____

_____

Ages

———————————

AGED
YEARS

———————————

this shall
That when

———————————

———————————

art

our

end

Mother   _gone_

glory

ELISABETH

rest

Thy

_____

_____

                    prayer
  when we

    we may

_____

_____

THING WITH FEATHERS

Celibacy: the name I call myself
        right as the birds wake:
                      no: what birds:

no birds but now I open
        the blinds: flies, large and silent:

        I'm so dulled, enfolded

    in the dread of being real
only to myself:
        the flies on the window won't move:

          mom on speaker phone:
                   one of the chickens got the taste
                      for its own eggs:

whose voice but mine
    interjects

        as I smash the flies
        with a hardback, one by one:

              poor bird, poor bird:

                  they splay open,
                    yellow inside:

        the book is by Zitkála-Šá:

just hit me, I said once to a man
        then struck my own cheek hard:

              felt myself warp and shrink:

before this peculiar experience I have no distinct memory
of having recognized any vital bond between myself and my own shadow,
wrote Zitkála-Šá:

o doubled form that no longer owns me:

        I fold into a paper towel
            the remains of these:

poor birds: what birds:

surely at some point my mind will cease
    reviving indignities:

    when the TSA agent slipped her
    fingers inside my waistband:

        moved slowly over
            my hip bones, the small
            of my back, my stomach:

                resting for a moment:

                      my gaze turned out and back
                          onto my body:

                    despite myself, turned on:

FIGURE [?]

The sickened flesh grown too aware of itself. Limbs touching limbs. Teeth grinding inside a closed mouth.

Proximity has everything to do with love: I become your face daily a new face. When we walk, the dog seems large or small. My mother mails me a packet of powdered broth.

No words for anything, not even when I was small, on the bench, overshadowed by eaves, pressing my back into the wall of my father's house. I wanted no one to look at me closely, my body, my face covered before the glory that was always there, glinting. I knew but didn't know what to call everything I knew what I wanted but was unable to say.

What actually survives the possibility, or impossibility of speaking. Late summer pollen between porch boards.

I heat water. I drink the broth. *Would that I had a past within me, I would possess all tomorrows.* Born in the shadow of a paper mill, I grew up there in the sulfur, billowing.

REMOVAL ACT

To vomit at will was my privilege.
Indoor plumbing was a must.

What smelled bad felt good. Vice versa.

It hurt at first
Then I got used to it:

The theme of womanly experience.

Rice could always be pushed to one side.
Ice cream stayed sweet on the way up.

I had too much time to think of who to be.

As Gertrude Stein said, of eating,
It was a shame it was a shame.

I liked to say, as if in wonder,

Ahhhh!
It made me sad and proud.

Slipped gear in my brain.
Rattle of the chain before the flush.

STATEMENT OF PURPOSE

I speak one language. I want another
English degree. Since childhood I haven't
settled anywhere due to poetry, in pursuit
of unread books unpacked again, stacked in
corners. Furniture left on a curb in the rain.
When Grandpa was young, he says, his father
sold their regalia so Esther could attend
secretary school. They lived in South Dakota.
Dakota, we call ourselves. *South*, positioning
one state below another, as I position myself
lifting a fringed shirt over my head, or in
a life typing what other people say. Next
paragraph.

Research interests, poetic lineage.
In the trunk of my car, a mildewed coat,
powder-green, for I live in a state with
damp air, where events begin with land
acknowledgments. That air interests me,
wetter than gray, and the austere silence
after thanking Indians broadly, as if none
were present. Fleeing a famine, he says,
they found here a one-room shack. And I,
seeking poetry, have found myself under
cheap bulbs, eschewing abstract words,
like *poetry*, for concrete ones, like *poem*.

Now a detail to pull the reader in,
teen me walking home in a red cardigan
stitched with the school crest, *Soli Deo
Gloria* on a banner, sleeves unraveling.
Life felt discretely mine and art—like love,

something perfect to be made in the future.
It interests me where things end up. Esther
was a typist for the Agency. Books become
Texts; Family becomes Provenance. I find
online, glass-cased, *Yankton Dakota Chief's
Outer Dress, Provenance Unknown*, draped on
a suggestion of human. I have, concretely.
My face in the mirror, settled light on itself.
Another poem opening with a first-person
declaration. I speak one language. I want
another English degree. In my car, that coat
I've left for months—how could I forget

      to step into his house, Dakota land,
a piece the size of a placard. He rises from
a recliner—*Oh, it's going along*—squeezes my
hands, asks where I'm moving, never why.
To have lived through so many omissions.
To be a sleeve, no arms inside. Yet I've
worked hard for this 4.0 in concrete details,
e.g., he stands in his suspenders and pilled
polyester gray pants, eyes spotted with dark
pools I peer into and through to . . .

      Did you like that? Did I please you? Do my
concerns reveal a clear thematic line? And
what do you think of my future? Is it bright?
Brain-bright like whip-smart or white-bright
proliferating sun, ray here, ray there, jagged
glare outside the glass case inside of which
I'm squinting, spores coating the surface of
my tongue and in the hollow of my mouth
I finally

00000000

I have desired most
to be desired

Last drops of juice
squeezed from the lime

Husked and thereafter
gone my givingness

•

Oh, handsome men!
I'm sick of them

The new girlfriends
look like me
or I look like
the old girlfriends

•

Their fathers
sell the missiles
their grandfathers
designed

drunk on
their wine
I slept warm
in their past

•

Now I'm brought
to consideration
of trust funds

    •

(*Not at all a proper subject for the lyric,* my teacher said)

    •

Nothing follows generations
like zeroes in bank accounts

and a resulting politeness
concerning origins

    •

Debt like a lyric
situation constrains

until having been
exited it once again
becomes illusory

    •

the similarities end there

    •

and yes I have desired
most some money
some money without trying

    •

more cushioned
than my mother's rage

her joy
a silent deep-sea creature
monstrous with its almost-human face

•

You (Fed Loan Servicing)
lifted delicate unagi
to my lips as I reclined
on a white leather sofa

•

I am all deferrals
and transfers now

•

My country climbs
an upward line
of militarized
spending

•

Last week depositing
a twenty-five dollar
check for a poem
from a state
university

I moved again
from object to subject
to subjection

reciting my ATM code
with my index
by heart

•

From blood
comes money
from blood

•

And you (Chase Bank)
put your arms around me
in your parents' summer
home and out French
doors I saw blue water

•

My country
makes up zeroes
every day

•

Still it all
and them
I wanted

•

But take me past
the moment of complicity
piss-warm pool of admission

•

There must be some
form of doing

some form of having done

Even privately

•

I want to have
done something

•

(See Figure I: as of yet empty)

•

Unthinkable to think
outside myself I

•

For twenty years, the nuclear launch code at US weapons silos was set to 00000000,
to minimize delay

•

My country
pervaded by
an inarticulable
lyric pressure

•

Small desire
small has it kept me

I shudder like a bad transmission

•

My country
occurred

occurs daily

both with
and without
my permission

•

The ease
with which I typed
that code

•

A missile also
is a situation

illusory

to every I
outside it

•

The lyric's
constrained

speaker's
small desire

•

The ease
the speed

One second
Less

Twenty-five dollars
Blue water

•

On the other side
of self-recognition
lies a secret
undulating form

that has followed me
for generations

•

Hereafter
I desire
to become

•

By heart
By heart
By heart

FIGURE [?]

I held anger for so long. At you as part of me and subject of me and object of something far bigger.

My father, reading lesser-known Milton. The past loved him more than it loved me. At the antique store in the repurposed sawmill a woman said to me, *I'd know that face anywhere. An assembly of history's traces deposited in me.*

Now I am older and nothing that worked for him works for me. Light: a thing a man makes. My father's father, the sheriff, striking a match on the zipper of his Levi's.

But I am also suspicious of confession. Once a week, I sharpen the knives. *The pacing of their experience intermittent.* Outgrowing my fetish for parallel syntax. A friend says to push my writing out of vaguely wistful tones.

What you're doing is lining up all kinds of footnotes. I want to write, "Mine are the heavens. A life in which everything holds significance can be very tiring, I think."

THE REAL THING

At the public park
        I cover my body
                with sunscreen

and sit on a towel
        in my Coca-Cola
                bikini, printed with

THE REAL THING!
        in cursive all over.
                Reading Rukeyser,

I'm seeking language
        behind my facade of
                language. Propped

on the hill, steel
        letters, fifty feet tall,
                declare the current

name for this place,
        previously El Pueblo
                de Nuestra Señora

la Reina de los Ángeles
        del Rio Porciúncula.
                Before that, Tovaangar.

Decades ago, the sign
        was briefly altered
                by an artist, sheets

of plastic revealing
        OIL WAR. If I look
               past the page: within

THE REAL, HERE
        sits next to THERE.
               In my hip's dent,

sweat pools, drowning
        the gnat that tried
               to traverse it.

INTERKINDNESSES

sidewalk narrows in dusk
two bushes grown over it
toward one another
me and

                  again on the phone

                               never told anyone
                               before tonight I

[   ]

binaural feedback behind words a low buzz

                               came back
                               in a rush

                leafless endings tangled
                in a knot scrap of candy
                wrapper flickering yellow
                flame caught in center

[   ]

when a matrix of pain is a matrix of care
well   I can hold my palm over a candle
longer than you'd think

I had to leave
the
room I

when those who were children have children
where doesn't the crying come from

don't know how
to fix

$$\left(\right) \begin{matrix} \rightarrow \\ \leftarrow \end{matrix} \left(\right)$$

after what happens happens   happens
to the one it happens to   to the one
what happens   after

pressed to my ear
origin of

what
I did what
I

sound waves arcing up and down
sunset's slowly muting shades
my attendant place

remember

no need
but for
a frame
to hold

REMOVAL ACT

All the while the dog was dying.
I didn't know. His little heaps

of yellow vomit. Damp spots
where he'd slept. I didn't know

what it meant until meaning
sat still enough for me to see

nothing else. Then a man put
in my hand a pamphlet on loss.

Big flat words. A sun, rising
or setting above gray waves,

the clouds arrayed in shapes
incomparable to any animal.

I thanked him. Shut the door.
For a long time, I lay quiet

on the floor. Unneeded, I
had no meaning. Or meaning

unmade itself, no longer
needing me.

FIGURE [?]

Applause first. Today, I made a great decision to never again. Today, I'm going to live and so is God. *What's living and breathing in the place hidden from view.*

I go to a building full of machines. Pulleys, springs. I swing my arms open and shut. Carrying tautness with me.

In other people's words I sought some sound to follow. In the peal of their perfect phrasing. To follow where. Embarrassing, this urge.

That poet I said is making a value judgment. *But no one has a monopoly on morality.* All my life I have mistaken self-preservation for wisdom. All I've made: one photo of the self with the face of the self obscured by the self's gaze.

May my embarrassments oft open me. Split halves of a peach and the knife between— one straight line. A clean wound, observed.

SCREENSHOTS

findagrave.com, database and images, memorial page for Elisabeth "Lizzie" Bercier Majhor

[Here, Elisabeth. Here,
in her portrait, taken
at Standing Rock.
And here, another photo
of a painting of her photo.
Unremarkable painting, I decide,
but faithful to its source:
broad brows arcing,
clumsy gleam dropped
in the center of each pupil.
Paintings are, in English, *made*,
while photos are *taken*.
Like care, pills, space.]

[I sat today, carefully
arranged, as a man angled
lights at my face.
No one's really looked at you,
he said. His camera made
honed and splendid
the feeling in my eyes,
feeling I *had*, in English,
like names, children, lunch.
I've never looked at, not really.
So unremarkable, my faithful—
in this rented room,
I took what I have and I made.]

[She was born in winter. In a place where November is winter. Snow on the ground, or too early for snow. Slow tongues. Thick tonsils. Hemlock boughs dragging. Hard dirt. Wet air on the surface of her eye when first she lifted lids and saw the face of her mother looming, half-shadowed. Partial moon. No thought yet of mother. No glimpse yet of moon. Curved pale outside. Barely above. Lids closing. Opening. A wail. Thumbs uncurling.]

[I'm here]

[But she is dead]

[In the sleigh, wrapped around her daughter wrapped around her baby. Unplumbed. Nose hairs cased in ice. Slowing hearts. Valentine's Day.]

[The miles between]

[Birth and death]

[Equalling the forced]

[Re]

[She would have been 16]

[Nails gnawed to skin. Arms crossed over her chest as she
walked. Eyes trained on dust rising up from the heels of
those before her, dust settling again on the road. Breath
of footsteps moving dust.]

[moval]

[A leather ribbon
silently loosening
from her hair
falling through cold
air curling over and
onto itself]

[On foot and in
wagons] [
Passing
identical]   [
Town after
town] [
Procession of]
[Dakota
prisoners]
      [Four
miles long]
      [
Abstracted to]
      [Dark
furrows]
[In that
landscape]
      [My
family does]
      [Not
speak about it]
[The soldiers
chained]

[Their
feet together]
      [Heads
covered]
[With blankets
]   [
Stomachs
empty]
      [
Throats parched
]
[Settlers
opened]
               [
Front doors]
      [Lined
the streets]
[Throwing]
               [
Rocks and
sticks
] [Tomatoes and
rotten eggs]

[We don't
really speak
 about it]
      [
Scalding water]
               [
Poured from]
[An open
window]
               [
From this great
distance]
Prisoners pulled
]   [
By long hair]
[From wagons
]   [
You can
imagine the
reasons]
      [Even a
baby]

[
Remember]
[Snatched from
its mother]
      [Dashed
to the ground]
      [The
face of anger] [
Contorting like
] [
The face of]
[   ]
      [Pain]
               [
A mother's
wails]   [
Rising]
[Washed away
]
      [With
river silt]
      [None
of us speak]

[What can I do]

    [Count breaths in her head]

    [Lift her eyes to see]

    [One-eyed rabbit]

    [Steam plume]

    [Bare barn]

    [Elk tracks]

    [Barbed wire]

    [Plowed furrows]

    [New snow]

        [Standing still while
        hills roll backward]

[Even as a child]   [I won every staring contest]

[One wagon a wooden wagon carrying elders and children had an ungreased
wheel without any spokes just a round board made a loud and squealing sound
the noise heard a mile away the noise never stopped as long as the wagon kept
moving they plugged their ears with their fingers their heads hurt from the
sound the sound continued as long as the movement never stopped]

[Who among you
will open your door]

[?]

[?]

[?]

[Who will come out]

[Behold her]

[Beholden]

[A Virgin of her]

[A Version]

[In the Cemetery of Assumptions]

[Blessed of the Blessed of the Blessed]

[I produced readily
poetry of death]

[Wrote a baby thrown
to the ground]

[Laid the image in
the crook of a tree]

[Crying mother
of that image]

[Another image
of suffering]

[*Erin, genocide sells*]

[Am I the loud
spokeless wheel]

[*Erin, what would
you write for us*]

[The leather ribbon

loosening yes and

silent falling from

her hair somewhere

sky stretched above

in the midst of her

turning a cartwheel

rising turning over

and onto herself]

[Now herself]

　　[Digitized]

　　　　[looks back] [At me]

　　　　[Eyes deepset beneath furrow]

　　　　[Arms holding a baby her baby]

　　　　　[Left hand falling across]

　　　　　[I almost make out]

　　　　　[A tiny hand] [?] [A toy] [?]

　　　　　　　[Baby so tightly
　　　　　　　pulled into]

　　　　　　　　[She cradles]

　　　　　　　　　[Full screen]

You stare square. Braids down from middle part. Strands escaping. Marks of material. Intervals. Shoulders. Deterioration. To not be able. You make me. Your eyes. While safety. Discomforted. I find your gaze also. Its silence. No not silence. Quiet. In shadows. Of light. All upon certain points. Settling pearlbright buttons. I cannot touch you.

in your arms baby. Baby of your dress. Most husbands. That is evidenced. Babys blond cut baby from the photo. Laying on a table. In this way. As anything other. At once all Those noisy bundles. My own disquiet. I to attempt. Your left hand across. Your supporting. I begin to hear. Full of a strong. you can. You cover as much. Insepar stare square. Braids down from escaping. Marks of material. rs. Deterioration. To no ke me. Your eyes. scomforted. I fin Its silence. No iet. In shadow upon certain pearlbrigh not touch ow   your n in your your   dress. th your wh at is evi blond aring.

Cannot know your mind. Unknown markedly. Both your white hairs. Baby staring. Were I to Would anyone look at baby. together. Measure of my. Another. Even quieter. Were right   arm.   Babys   head With your open hand. As able. I cannot quite. You middle part. Strands Intervals.   Shoulde t be able. You ma While safety. Di d your gaze also. not silence. Qu s. Of light. All points. Settling t buttons. I can you. Cannot kn mind. Unknow arms baby. Baby of Most markedly. Bo ite husbands. Th denced. Babys hairs. Baby st Were I to cut

baby from the photo. Laying on a table. Would anyone look at baby. In this way. As anything other. At once all together. Measure of my. Those noisy bundles. My own disquiet. Another. Even quieter. Were I to attempt. Your left hand across. Your right arm. Babys head supporting. I begin to hear. Full

[Each time I screenshot]

[A shutter sound]

[Before]

                        [Beneath black hood]

                           [Head looming]

                             [One arm waving]

                                 [Fingers snapping]

                                     [Baby's head swiveling]

                                     [That sound]

                                [Thumbs uncurling]

                           [Remain uncaptured]

                       [Hood pushed back]

                   [Head emerging smiling]

             [Baby clapping hands]

[After]

In their memory
plant memorial trees

[When grandpa dropped a manila folder
contents scattering across the floor
on the tile your face your eyes
the ancient chihuahua's nails
clicked across your mouth
and you were elsewhere]

[In all your life's movements] [Exceeding] [That all-knowing shutter] [All the churning of cream to butter] [Steady thumping to the beat of your heart] [All the wading in the creek and the catching of crawdads in skunk cabbage leaves] [Your skirt hiked above the knee] [Knees knobby] [Knees clean] [All the crawdads boiled scarlet] [Feelers curling like ribbon] [All the blood flowing from your nostrils in summer heat] [All the sweat distilled against your brow] [All the yelling and the weight of head on shoulder after] [All the brushing of cattails soft against your palm] [All the ragweed spreading] [All the coarse coughs] [In the currents of the air] [All the tin pails] [The clear water] [The wet rags dripping] [All the card games, the deck marked with soot, bearing an armored knight caught in thorns and the queen of diamonds gazing sidelong, pinching a four-pointed flower, her crown bent on one edge so you knew when she was drawn] [All the circles traced with your toe in the dirt] [All the songs full of quick breaths between long vowels] [All the scents of the horses in the stable] [Their heavy chests after running] [All the canvas bags distended with feed] [All the acres of soil stretching] [All the seeds in the fresh-plowed acres] [And all the weather waiting] [In the clouds' hardened furrows] [Hard with heat] [Humming]

[Year after

year your lost

leather ribbon

lay where you

left it turning

into ground]

[Eyes tired, I close]

[The laptop screen]

[Look, it's still light]

[Hear a plane hum]

[Its motion writing]

[For us soft letters]

A   N   D

[Within the frame]

[That limits me]

[To future forms]

[I leave myself]

NOTES

"To This I Come" and "Screenshots": My imperfect understanding of the tribal histories of the US-Dakota War of 1862 and its aftermath is drawn from the knowledge, writing, and thinking of Dakota scholars and writers, most notably Waziyatawin, Chris Mato Nunpa, and Gwen Nell Westerman. I thank them.

"Removal Act": The portrait of Mato Sabi Ceya can be found in Album 39 of the William Blackmore Collection, currently held in the British Museum. The Yankton Treaty, signed in 1858, ceded eleven million acres to the US government and opened that land up to settlers.

"8.5 x 11": The Adrian Piper line comes from her essay "Passing for White, Passing for Black." *Gather* is the documentary referenced in this poem.

"From the Archive of American Object Lessons": The names of these tribes appear here as they were spelled in the original legislative act.

"To Go There": This poem ends with an altered page from Layli Long Soldier's *WHEREAS*. I have included both Layli Long Soldier's lines and a paragraph that she "lifted" from Zitkála-Šá's *Impressions of an Indian Childhood*, then redacted with single-line strikethroughs. Layli Long Soldier's words are signaled here by italics. Double-line strikethroughs and bracketed additions are my own.

"Epigenesis": The phrase "psychic and consequently physical" comes from the essay "Who Is Your Mother? Red Roots of White Feminism" by Paula Gunn Allen. On page 46, I have transcribed the recording of the conversation as it occurred. In actuality, Sitting Bull was killed two weeks before the massacre at Wounded Knee.

"Thing with Feathers": A sentence is taken from Zitkála-Šá's *Impressions of an Indian Childhood*. The title of this poem comes from Emily Dickinson's line "'Hope' is the thing with feathers -."

"Removal Act": The Gertrude Stein quote is found in *Tender Buttons*.

"Screenshots": Find a Grave, a subsidiary of Ancestry.com, is the largest database of cemetery records in the world. Designed to provide a "virtual cemetery experience," the website is updated by volunteer members, who upload photos and biographical information to virtual memorial pages. The video stills at the end of this poem come from a video I made of myself putting on and taking off my great-grandmother Lorena's Camp Fire Girls dress.

"Figure [?]": The following authors and texts are quoted in these poems, listed here in the order that the reader encounters them:

Paula Gunn Allen, "Who Is Your Mother? Red Roots of White Feminism"
Bhanu Kapil, *The Vertical Interrogation of Strangers*
Gilles Deleuze and Felix Guattari, *A Thousand Plateaus*
Waziyatawin, "A Journey of Healing and Awakening"
M. NourbeSe Philip, *Zong!: As Told to the Author by Setaey Adamu Boateng*
Amiri Baraka, "As a Possible Lover"
Julia Kristeva, *Powers of Horror*
Fred Moten and Stefano Harney, *The Undercommons: Fugitive Planning & Black Study*
Hone Tūwhare, "Rain"
Sheila Heti, *Motherhood*
Maria Yellow Horse Brave Heart, "Historical Trauma and Unresolved Grief: Implications for Clinical Research and Practice with Indigenous Peoples of the Americas"
Giorgio Agamben, "The Archive and Testimony"
Mahmoud Darwish, "Ivory Combs"
Julietta Singh, *No Archive Will Restore You*
Lauren Berlant, "Slow Death (Sovereignty, Obesity, Lateral Agency)"
Vine Deloria, Jr., "A Conversation with Vine Deloria, Jr."
Avery F. Gordon, *Ghostly Matters: Haunting and the Sociological Imagination*
June Jordan, "Creation Is Revolutionary," 1978 interview with Karla Hammond in *Kalliope*

ACKNOWLEDGMENTS

I'm grateful to the publications in which earlier versions of these poems first appeared: the *Adroit Journal, Beloit Poetry Journal, Best New Poets, Chapter House, DIAGRAM, Narrative,* and *Poetry Northwest.*

Thank you to every classmate and friend who read these poems, talked with me about writing, or otherwise gave to this book: Gabrielle Bates, Patrycja Humienik, Erin L. McCoy, Alexandria Hall, Tom Renjilian, Michelle Orsi, Amelia Ada, Laura Roque, Jonathan Escoffery, Leesa Fenderson, Jonathan Leal, Taneum Bambrick, Aria Aber, James Ciano, Bryan Byrdlong, Mitchell Jacobs, Leah Tieger, Ashley Dailey, Marcus Clayton, Melissa Chadburn, Cameron Lange, Austen Rosenfeld, Catherine Pond, Matt Jones, Elizabeth Schiffler, Izzi Vasquez, Max Delsohn, D. A. Navoti, Nia Dickens, Lisa Levin, Luke Heister, Sarah Ridley, and countless others.

I have been very fortunate to receive support from many teachers over the years, especially Chris Finley, Nancy Marie Mithlo, Susan McCabe, Pimone Triplett, Dana Johnson, and Danzy Senna. A special thank you to David St. John for making this reality possible.

Thank you to Cameron Coffman for expert editing of video stills, and to Panos Kokkinias for generous use of the photograph that appears in the background. Thank you to Jonathan Chacón for the author portrait.

Thank you to Samantha Majhor for talking through the finer points of our family history. And thank you to Alison Rath, my Oneida sister, for the ongoing conversations and insights.

I am forever grateful to Chantz Erolin for seeing potential in this manuscript, asking for more, and giving patient, perceptive edits. Thank you to Jeff Shotts, Katie Dublinski, and Carmen Giménez for their support and guidance. Gratitude, also, to the rest of the Graywolf team for their welcoming kindness and all their labor, seen and unseen.

To my mother and father, Ann and Bryan, for the education and the steadfast love. To my grandfather, Bob, for the stories and the responsibility. And to the rest of my family, both with me and in spirit.

ERIN MARIE LYNCH is a PhD candidate in creative writing and literature at the University of Southern California. A 2023 NEA Creative Writing Fellow, her work appears in *Gulf Coast*, *DIAGRAM*, *Best New Poets*, and elsewhere.

The text of *Removal Acts* is set in Adobe Garamond Pro.
Book design by Rachel Holscher.
Composition by Bookmobile Design and Digital
Publisher Services, Minneapolis, Minnesota.
Manufactured by Versa Press on acid-free,
30 percent postconsumer wastepaper.